A BOOK TO BEGIN ON

THE CIRCUS

By Mary Kay Phelan   Illustrated by John Alcorn

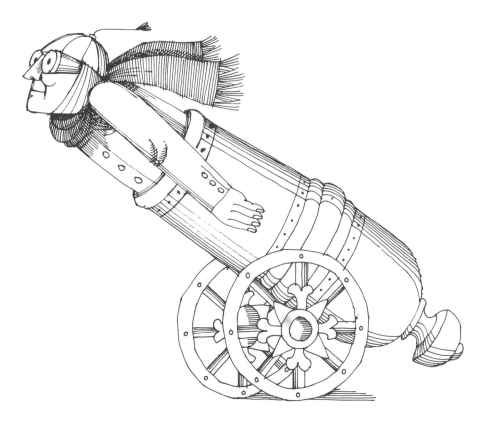

HOLT, RINEHART AND WINSTON

New York / Chicago / San Francisco

FIRST EDITION

Library of Congress Catalog Card Number 63–9083

97047-0313
Printed in the United States of America

The circus is coming! The circus is coming!

For years these have been magic words to boys and girls all over America. Some children think of a circus on television with dancing elephants and funny clowns. Others remember the high-wire acts way up under the top of the big tent.

But to almost everyone, the circus is more exciting than fireworks on the Fourth of July!

No one knows exactly when the circus began. Some people say it began on the island of Crete in the Mediterranean Sea, about four thousand years ago.

Boys and girls were trained to do a bull-leaping act. When an angry bull charged, the leaper grabbed its horns. Then he flipped over the bull's back, landing on his feet behind the animal.

This daring act may have been the first circus stunt in the world.

The circus we now watch began with the Circus Maximus in ancient Rome. In Latin, *circus* means circle. *Maximus* means great.

The Romans built a great circle of seats, where many thousands of people could sit.

This circus started with a big parade. Then came chariot races. Acrobats and jugglers did stunts. Sometimes men called gladiators fought other men or wild animals.

There was always great excitement at the Circus Maximus.

For almost a thousand years people went to the Circus Maximus. Then some countries began to make war on Rome. There was no more time for a circus in the great circle.

But still people liked to be amused. The acrobats and jugglers knew that people would pay money to see their stunts.

When they could no longer perform in Rome, they began to wander all over Europe. Two or three performers would travel together. They did tricks on street corners and people tossed coins to reward them.

Although there was no real circus as yet, the acrobats and jugglers were keeping the idea of a circus alive. At the same time, fairs were being held all over Europe.

The first fairs began when people gathered at a church on a saint's day. Before long, jugglers and acrobats came to amuse the people outside the church.

Perhaps the most famous of all fairs was one held in England. It was called St. Bartholemew's Fair. It began in 1123. Only the best acrobats and jugglers were asked to perform there.

Several hundred years passed. The fairs grew larger and larger. More stunt men came to do tricks. Some even brought strange animals to show to people.

Then, in 1770, an Englishman, Philip Astley, tried something new. He opened a riding ring in London. People sat in seats all around the ring, while Astley did tricks on his horse. Later, he added a clown, a ropewalker, and acrobats.

Philip Astley is often called the "Father of the Circus," because he used a riding ring for his acts.

Mr. Astley was so successful with his London circus that others tried the same idea in all parts of Europe.

Soon, Antonio Franconi opened a circus in Paris. His sons joined him—and then his grandsons. The Franconi family became famous for their riding tricks performed on dancing horses.

Meanwhile, many people from Europe had moved to the New World. Among the first settlers in America were men who trapped wild animals and sold their furs.

Sometimes one of these trappers would tame a wild bear. Then he would take it to the nearest village. And the bear would do tricks for anyone who would watch.

This was the beginning of circus acts in America.

More and more people were coming to the New World. Ships were sailing back and forth across the Atlantic Ocean. Once in a while a ship's captain would buy a strange animal and bring it back to show in America.

The first lion arrived here in 1770. People said they had never seen anything like it.

In 1792, a Scotchman, John Bill Ricketts, arrived in America. Mr. Ricketts had learned trick riding in England. He settled in Philadelphia, and opened the first circus there on April 3, 1793. George Washington, our first president, was watching.

The circus had a clown and a tightrope walker. But the main act was trick riding. On his horse, Cornplanter, Mr. Ricketts made a flying leap over the back of another horse.

To John Bill Ricketts goes the honor of presenting the first complete American circus.

For many years, every outdoor circus
has had "side shows." Small tents are set
up near the big one. In each tent there is
something special for visitors to see.

John Bill Ricketts started this custom
when he bought a white charger named
Jack. This was the horse President
Washington had ridden during the
Revolutionary War.

The famous white horse was shown in a
special stall at Ricketts' circus. This was
the first side show in the first American
circus.

In 1776, Captain Jacob Crowinshield sailed his ship into New York harbor. On board was a strange new animal which the Captain had bought in India. This was the first elephant ever to set foot in America.

Little did Captain Crowinshield know how important the elephant would become in the circus.

Years later, people began counting elephants whenever the circus paraded into town. The more elephants they could count, the bigger the circus would be.

It was an elephant, too, that started the traveling circus in America.

In 1815, a sea captain brought "Old Bet," an African elephant, to this country. The captain's brother, Hachaliah Bailey, bought "Old Bet."

Then Mr. Bailey walked the huge animal around the countryside, showing her in farmers' barns. Mr. Bailey and his elephant always traveled after dark, so no one could get a free look.

Mr. Bailey did so well showing "Old Bet" that he added more animals to his traveling show.

Several of Mr. Bailey's neighbors thought this was a good idea. *They* bought animals and traveled about the countryside, too. Some even had clowns and trick riders.

By 1820, there were about thirty shows traveling in wagons. They all came from Mr. Bailey's neighborhood near Somers, New York. This area became known as the "Cradle of the American Circus."

As the pioneers began to move West, the circus followed. There was little to do for entertainment in this backwoods country. Everyone looked forward to Circus Day.

The shows traveled in wagons along rough country roads. Sometimes the mud along the roads was very deep.

Because the circus had to travel through so much mud, it was soon nicknamed "the mud show."

About a week before the mud show arrived, a horseback rider would gallop into town. He would nail up big signs telling about the circus.

Sometimes he would walk up and down the muddy streets, ringing a bell and shouting that the circus was coming to town.

Two hours before the circus arrived, a jolly clown would bound into the town square.

He did tricks to make children laugh. He told all about the wonders in the circus.

And finally he announced the starting time for the big show.

The circus would roll into town in red-painted wagons.

A wall of canvas would be set up in a circle. Tickets were twenty-five cents and people had to stand while they watched the circus.

Shows were held in the afternoon. Even a gentle little breeze would blow out the candles used for lighting at night.

Wind or rain could ruin a mud show. But in 1830, a circus manager, Aaron Turner, found the answer to this problem. He invented a round-top tent. No matter what the weather was like, Turner's circus could always give its performances.

Every outdoor circus since that day has performed under a tent, now called the "Big Top."

No circus is ever complete without the funny-faced clowns that make children—and grown ups—laugh.

The first clown to become a great star was Joey Grimaldi. He performed in London in the early 1800's. Ever since then, circus clowns have always been called "joeys."

Once a clown decides how he wants to paint his face, that face becomes his "trade mark." No other clown ever copies it.

America's first great clown was Dan Rice. He grew whiskers and wore a red-and-white-striped costume that looked a little like the American flag.

In his act, Dan Rice used a pig called Lord Byron. When the clown asked Lord Byron a question, the pig answered by grunting "oink, oink" at the right time.

At the end of the act, Rice would give Lord Byron a box filled with the flags of many countries. The pig always picked out the American flag and waved it at the crowd.

There were not only famous clowns. There were also men who became famous as circus owners. One famous owner was Gilbert Spalding.

Mr. Spalding had many ideas about how to make his circus better. He used oil lamps instead of candles to light his tent. He invented a special kind of bleachers to seat the audience. And he was the first owner to move his circus by railroad instead of by wagons.

But Gilbert Spalding is best remembered for his beautiful Floating Palace which began its travels in 1852. This was a huge barge painted cream and gold. It was pulled by two towboats.

Inside the Floating Palace was a large circus ring. Around the ring were seats for more than two thousand people.

The boat traveled up and down the Mississippi River, stopping along the way to give shows at all the small towns.

Another famous name in circus history was Phineas Taylor Barnum. He would do anything to fool people. Sometimes he was called the "Prince of Humbugs."

For thirty years P.T. Barnum had a museum in New York City. He collected strange looking people and things called freaks from all over the world. He put them in his museum. People brought lunch baskets and stayed all day, just looking at the odd sights.

The most famous sight at Barnum's American Museum was a midget named Charles S. Stratton. This midget was only twenty-five inches tall; he weighed fifteen pounds. Barnum called him "General Tom Thumb."

Another one of the exhibits was the Giant Baby. He was seven years old and weighed two hundred and fifty-seven pounds.

Barnum's museum was very different from the museums we know today. It was more like the side shows at the circus.

In 1870, P.T. Barnum was sixty years old. His museum had burned down, but Barnum had enough money so that he didn't have to work.

Then William Cameron Coup, owner of a big circus, went to Mr. Barnum and asked him to be a partner in Coup's Circus. Barnum liked the idea.

On April 10, 1871, the Barnum and Coup Circus opened in Brooklyn, New York, under the largest tent people had ever seen. A year later, the circus was traveling all over the country in more than seventy railroad cars.

But Barnum and Coup could not get along well together. After several years they decided they would no longer be partners.

Meanwhile, other big circuses were traveling around the country. One of these belonged to James A. Bailey. His show had both circus acts and a wild animal exhibit.

Bailey used the first electric lights in a circus. Thousands of people came to the show just to see this strange new invention.

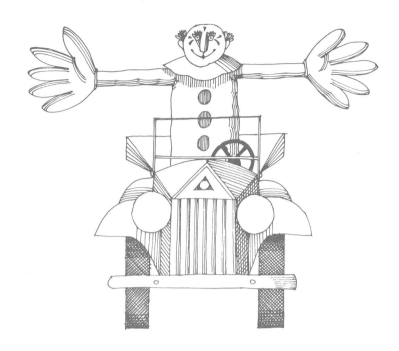

In 1881, Barnum and Bailey decided to join their circuses. Instead of one ring or two rings, they now had a three-ring circus. This was the first three-ring circus in America.

Several years later, a brand-new invention — the automobile — led the Barnum and Bailey circus parade. Some people said that the circus was just where the automobile belonged. No one would ever ride in such a crazy machine.

The most famous animal in the Barnum and Bailey Circus was Jumbo, the elephant. In 1882, P.T. Barnum bought him from the London Zoo.

Thousands and thousands of children came to the circus just to see the biggest elephant in America. Many of them rode on his back.

Jumbo was so famous that his name became part of our language. Today, anything that is much larger than usual is called jumbo-size.

In 1883, a new kind of circus was started. Buffalo Bill Cody, the famous Indian fighter, army scout, and buffalo hunter, opened the first Wild West Show. He had trick riders, sharpshooters, and Indians who fought cowboys in his show.

Buffalo Bill's best sharpshooter was Annie Oakley. She was called "Little Sure Shot." Lying on the back of a galloping horse, Annie shot down glass balls as they were tossed in the air by a circus helper. She did many other stunts, but this was her most difficult one.

Buffalo Bill's circus traveled by train, just as many circuses did. But others traveled by boat up and down the Mississippi River.

On circus day, all the boys in town gathered at the dock before dawn. Then they watched the circus unload and set up its show in a nearby field.

In the spring of 1869, the Dan Rice Circus docked at MacGregor, Iowa. Five little boys watched in wide-eyed wonder. They were Al, Otto, Charles, Alf T., and John Ringling.

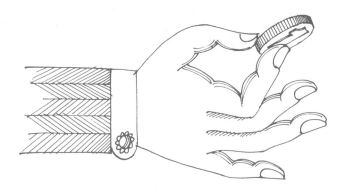

After seeing the circus, the Ringling boys decided to put on a show in their own back yard. The admission price was ten pins.

Later, the boys added an old billy goat, which they called "Billy Rainbow." Now it cost one cent to see the Ringling Brothers' Circus.

The five Ringlings were very serious about the circus business. They learned to do tricks. They saved every penny to buy wagons and a tent.

Just thirteen years after seeing their first circus, the Ringlings took their own show out on the road.

Later, two more brothers, Gus and Henry, joined the family business. All seven brothers worked very hard.

During the next few years the Ringling Brothers kept buying more and more circuses. By 1922, they had bought all the big circuses in America, including Barnum and Bailey. Now they were known as the "Greatest Show on Earth."

One hundred railroad cars were needed to move the Ringling Brothers and Barnum and Bailey Circus from one town to another.

Several weeks before the Ringling Brothers' Circus arrived, the "advance men" came to town and rented some land where the circus would perform.

The "bill posters" came next. These were men who tacked up big signs telling all about the circus.

The circus usually arrived long before dawn. The equipment was unloaded. The tents were set up.

The first tent to go up was called the "cookhouse." This was where circus people ate. When the meal was ready, a flag was flown from the top of the tent.

Next, the animal tents and the tents for the side shows were put up. Last of all came the "Big Top," where the circus was held.

Small boys in the town were hired to help. Some carried water for elephants. Others did odd jobs. Circus people called these boys "punks." Their pay was a free ticket to the big show.

Everyone in town turned out for the circus parade in the morning.

Down the main street came lovely ladies on prancing horses. Next came the band in red-and-gold uniforms, riding on a beautiful band wagon.

Cages of wild animals and a long line of elephants followed. Clowns, riding goats or driving funny old cars, would weave in and out of the long parade.

At the end of the procession was the steam calliope. Its shrill music meant that the parade was over.

The crowd began to gather at the circus ground soon after lunch. People bought their tickets at the ticket wagon and then wandered around looking at the cages of wild animals.

Some bought popcorn and cotton candy. Others went into the small tents to see the side shows.

One side show had "the fattest lady in the world." Another had a man who ate fire. In still another was a man who swallowed a sharp sword.

The magic moment drew nearer. People began taking their seats under the Big Top.

Into the center ring stepped the red-coated ringmaster. The band struck up and the "Grand Entry" began. All the performers marched around the ring.

When the parade was over, the ringmaster blew one sharp blast on his whistle. All three rings came alive!

There were leaping horses, with lovely ladies riding bareback on them. There were trained seals, waltzing elephants, and wild animal acts.

Clowns were everywhere. They chased pigs, fell out of old cars, and tripped over their own big shoes.

There were daring high-wire acts and flying-trapeze stunts—each one more exciting than the last.

All too soon, the big show was over. Before long the circus would be moving on to the next town.

Today, most circuses are held in big buildings.

There are only a few of the "tent shows" left. But as long as there are boys and girls—and grown ups—to laugh at the clowns, throw peanuts to the elephants, and shriek with excitement when the high-wire artists whirl through the air, there will always be a circus!

MARY KAY PHELAN lives in Davenport, Iowa, where she aids her husband in the editing of historical films produced by his company. The mother of two boys, Mrs. Phelan graduated from De Pauw University, and holds an M.A. from Northwestern University.

The excitement and color of the circus has always been a source of fascination for Mrs. Phelan, so that when a third-grade neighbor suggested that she write a book about it, she started work immediately. THE CIRCUS is Mrs. Phelan's second Book to Begin On; she is also the author of *The White House.*

JOHN ALCORN, a native New Yorker, graduated from Cooper Union in 1955. An early member of the Push Pin Studios, he joined the Columbia Broadcasting System in 1958, but left there in 1960 to devote himself entirely to free-lance design and illustration. Recently turning his talents to books, he has illustrated a collection of Ogden Nash's verses and four books for children. *Books,* which he designed in 1962, was chosen by the New York *Times* as one of the ten best-illustrated children's books of that year. He has received awards from the Art Director's Club, the Society of Illustrators, the AIGA, and the Type Director's Club.

Mr. Alcorn, his wife, and their four young boys live in a two-hundred-and-thirty-year-old house in Ossining, New York.